100 Great Breads
Paul Hollywood

Photographs by Neil Barclay

CASSELL
ILLUSTRATED

An Hachette UK Company
www.hachette.co.uk

First published in Great Britain in 2004 by Cassell Illustrated,
a division of Octopus Publishing Group Ltd
Endeavour House, 189 Shaftesbury Avenue, London WC2H 8JY

This edition published in Great Britain in 2011

Edited by Victoria Alers-Hankey and Barbara Dixon
Photographs by Neil Barclay
Styled by Fanny Ward
Design by DW Design
Jacket design by Jo Knowles

ISBN: 978-1-8440-3700-1

Printed and bound in Italy

10   9   8   7   6   5   4

Acknowledgements

This book is dedicated to my wife, Alexandra, and my special boy, Joshua.

I would like to thank my mother, Gill, and father, John, for encouraging me into the baking trade in the first place and for washing endless mountains of chef's whites. I'd also like to thank my mother-in-law, Gloria, for helping me with some great recipe ideas.

Above all, a special thank you to my wife, Alexandra, for her support, love and patience during my career and the writing of this book.

Contents

Introduction

Bread is the one natural food that has been with us for centuries, but in recent years it has taken a back seat while we indulged our passion for fast foods bursting with additives and E numbers.

I grew up in Liverpool, the oldest of three boys, and food to us was just a source of energy. It wasn't until I began to make bread in my father's bakery that I realized that the variations and different types of bread were endless and that bread was not just the thick, white, sliced stuff to make bacon butties with!

The aroma of freshly baked bread evokes feelings and memories in all of us – a snug kitchen in the winter after school and a still-warm loaf on the table waiting to be smothered in butter and home-made strawberry jam is one of my favourites, but who can resist ciabatta straight from the oven, stuffed with glossy black olives, garlic and fresh coriander? Close your eyes and you're sitting on a vine-covered, sun-drenched terrace, sipping a glass of rich, red wine and surrounded by friends and family.

All the recipes in this book have special memories for me; some are from my childhood and some were discovered during my travels abroad. The textures and flavours all vary greatly, reflecting their origins, and I have added something of myself to all these recipes to make them unique and, I hope, satisfying to recreate.

Baking bread is a very sociable experience – you will find the whole family crowding into your kitchen, drawn by the irresistible fragrance of salmon brioche or a potato and rosemary focaccia. So pull up the chairs, break open a bottle and enjoy the novel experience of eating a home-baked loaf of bread.

Tools, Techniques and Tips

Tools

There are only a few tools needed to make a good loaf:

1. Baking trays and loaf tins

Any 450 g/1 lb traditional loaf tin is ideal for making breads. There are several varieties available, from Teflon to non-stick; some tins have straight sides, while others, such as farmhouse tins, tend to be more rounded.

Do remember to grease the tins – I use olive oil – before putting the dough in as this will ensure that the bread doesn't stick.

Baking trays are lined throughout – I line my trays with silicone paper or baking parchment. Greaseproof paper tends to stick.

2. Ovens

I have made bread in or on every oven imaginable, from open-flame to fan-assisted to range cookers; all are great for baking bread. Every oven has a character, especially in professional bakeries, and hot spots are common. Be aware of your oven as it may have these elusive hotspots; use them when baking and remember to turn your bread if the oven is a little hot at the back – the main reason for ovens being especially hot at the back is because over-impatient bakers look in the oven too often.

Most of the recipes in this book need oven temperatures between 200°–220°C/400°–425°F/mark 6–7. This is more than enough heat to bake bread; most industrial bakeries bake at 250°C/475°F/mark 9+, the main reason being to keep moisture in the loaf. The longer a loaf takes to colour or bake the drier it will be.

3. A good serrated knife or a sharp blade

I have no preferences with the knives that I use – any will do, but just remember to keep them sharp: the cut on the bread is very important, not only for the look, but for the crumb texture.

Techniques

Yeast

There are two main types of yeast available in the supermarkets today – dried and instant. Using dried yeast makes more work for yourself because you have to add water and sugar and leave it to froth. Instant yeast is more user-friendly because you literally throw it straight into the flour. However, be aware that this is a concentrated yeast and you will need less of it. All the recipes in this book use fresh yeast, but I would suggest you use instant yeast if you can't obtain fresh – if you use instant or dried then use 25 per cent less than the recipe states. Fresh yeast is available from most supermarkets nowadays – ask at the bakery department for a small amount and more often than not they will sell it to you. Failing that, ask at your local bakery.

Remember: all recipes use fresh yeast, so if you are using instant or dried yeast, reduce the quantities a little.

Mixing the ingredients for the dough

When mixing the ingredients, avoid contact between the yeast and salt: salt kills yeast, which means the bread won't rise.

Kneading

Kneading is an important part of bread making. The way I knead is very simple: start by making an indentation with the palms of your

hands into the middle of the dough – not too deep – then lift up the dough at the top and press it into the hole you have just made. Turn the dough and repeat and keep repeating this process for the length of time stated in the recipe. The kneading times I give may fluctuate by 2 minutes each way as you get more proficient.

Adding flavourings to the dough

Always add any flavourings after the dough has been kneaded and rested for at least 1 hour as this helps the dough to stabilize before being pumped with any additions.

When adding ingredients such as onions and garlic – ingredients that are intrinsically acidic – do not add too much as this retards or slows down the rising of the dough.

Tips

- Use this book as a base, but try incorporating your own ingredients and experiment with flavours and textures.

- You do not always need to dissolve yeast in warm water, just lob it in.

- You do not always need to use warm water when making bread, the bread will rise anyway, even in the fridge. The slower the rising (proving) time the more flavour the bread will have.

- The recipes in this book have measured water contents, but flours differ, so you may need a little extra water or a little less.

- When rolling out and kneading the dough, do not coat the table in inches of flour. The dough will pick it up and tighten up too much.

- I do not normally cover the dough when it is resting; a little skinning on the top should be incorporated back into the dough.

- Always preheat your oven so that your bread has somewhere to go when it is ready and not you!

- None of the breads in this book require steam or pots of water in the oven, I like the crusty earthy look of home-baked bread – there's nothing better.

- I put most of my breads onto a cooling rack when they come out of the oven – this is to prevent the bread from sweating and going soft.

- Do not store baked bread in a fridge – it will go stale three times quicker than if left in a bread bin.

Basic Breads

This earthy, hearty, full-flavoured loaf is from Eastern Europe. It will take up to 30 per cent more water than most bread doughs. The recipe uses rye baskets – they can be bought in basketware shops or ordered through the Internet.

I've tweaked this recipe over the years and am finally proud of it. It's gorgeous served fresh from the oven with lots of butter.

Dark Rye Bread *Illustrated*

Irish Soda Bread

350 g/12 oz dark rye flour, plus extra for dusting

150 g/5 oz wholemeal flour

1½ teaspoons salt

20 g/¾ oz yeast

4 tablespoons malt extract

2 tablespoons treacle

385 ml/13½ fl oz water

2 teaspoons cumin seeds

Makes 2 small loaves

Put 175 g/6 oz of rye flour and 75 g/ 3 oz of wholemeal flour into a bowl, then stir in the salt, yeast, malt extract and treacle and 150 ml/¼ pint of the water. Mix well for 5 minutes, then leave in the bowl to rise for 5 hours.

Line a baking tray. Add the remaining flours and water and the cumin seeds to the dough and mix well. Tip out onto a lightly floured surface, divide the dough into two and shape each into an oblong sausage. Coat each sausage with rye flour, place each in a rye basket and leave to rise for 2–3 hours.

Preheat the oven to 220°C/425°F/ mark 7. Tip each loaf out onto the baking tray and bake in the oven for 35 minutes, then transfer to a wire rack to cool.

500 g/1 lb 2 oz strong white flour, plus extra for dusting

20 g/¾ oz baking powder

1 teaspoon salt

75 g/3 oz butter, softened

200 ml/¼ pint buttermilk

150 ml/¼ pint milk

Makes 2 loaves

Put the flour, baking powder and salt into a bowl and work in the butter. Stir in the remaining ingredients and mix well.

Line a baking tray. Combine the mixture with your hands to make a dough, then divide the dough into two and shape into balls. Flatten the balls out and cut crosses in the top of each, then put on the baking tray and leave to rest for 20 minutes.

Preheat the oven to 200°C/400°F/ mark 6. Dust the dough lightly with flour and bake in the oven for 30–40 minutes. Transfer to a wire rack to cool.

I first ate this bread, baked for me by monks, while staying in Roscrea Monastery in Ireland.

A nice twist on the traditional bread, and tastes fantastic!

Wholemeal Soda Bread *Illustrated*

250 g/9 oz strong white flour, plus extra for dusting

250 g/9 oz wholemeal flour

20 g/¾ oz baking powder

1 teaspoon salt

75 g/3 oz butter, softened

270 ml/9 fl oz milk

30 ml/1 fl oz buttermilk

Makes 1 loaf

Preheat the oven to 200°C/400°F/ mark 6. Line a baking tray. Put all the ingredients into a large bowl and work together to form a soft dough. Shape into a ball and flatten slightly and cut a cross into the top, then dust the top with a little flour.

Put onto the baking tray and bake for 25 minutes until golden brown. Transfer to a wire rack to cool.

Variation: This bread can be made with 100 per cent white flour – just replace the wholemeal flour with 250 g/9 oz of white flour. Proceed as above.

Cheese and Onion Soda Bread

500 g/1 lb 2 oz strong white flour, plus extra for dusting

1½ teaspoons salt

300 ml/½ pint buttermilk

75 g/3 oz butter, softened

20 g/¾ oz baking powder

1 onion, peeled and finely chopped

75 g/3 oz Cheddar cheese, grated

Makes 2 loaves

Preheat the oven to 220°C/425°F/ mark 7. Line a baking tray. Put all the ingredients except the onion and cheese in a food mixer and, using a paddle blade and medium speed, blend together for 2 minutes. Alternatively, put into a bowl and mix well by hand for 5 minutes. Add the onion and cheese and incorporate, either by hand or in the mixer (don't overmix), into the dough.

Divide the dough into two pieces and tip out onto a lightly floured surface. Shape each piece into a ball, then flatten each with your hand so they are approximately 5 cm/2 inches thick. Cut a deep cross into each, dust with a little flour and put on the baking tray.

Bake for 30 minutes, then serve warm.

then transfer to a wire rack to cool.

French Breads

The French are passionate about their bread – historically, the shaving of bakers' heads for selling underweight bread was not uncommon. This loaf typifies French bread – a big, bold, hearty loaf full of flavour. Serve toasted or with cheese, it's a must try!

The ubiquitous baguette, filled with cheese and ham then toasted, is my lunch any day. Serve with a glass of chilled Chablis. Start this bread the day before.

Pain de Campagne *Illustrated*

Baguette

400 g/14 oz strong white flour, plus extra for dusting

100 g/3½ oz rye flour

10 g/¼ oz salt

20 g/¾ oz yeast

50 g/2 oz butter, softened

1 large bunch fresh oregano, destalked and chopped

300 ml/½ pint water

Makes 1 loaf

Put all the ingredients except the water into a bowl, then slowly add the water and mix in with your hands until all the flour on the sides of the bowl has been incorporated.

Tip the dough out onto a lightly floured surface and knead for 6 minutes. Put the dough back in the bowl and leave for 2 hours.

Line a baking tray. Tip the dough out onto your floured surface and shape into a ball, then slightly flatten with your hands and dust with flour. Using a knife, mark out a square shape on top of the dough, put on the baking tray and leave to rise for 1 hour.

Preheat the oven to 220°C/425°F/ mark 7. Bake for 30 minutes until golden brown, then transfer to a wire rack to cool.

500 g/1 lb 2 oz strong white flour

20 g/¾ oz yeast

warm water to mix

10 g/¼ oz salt

50 g/2 oz butter, softened

Makes 1 loaf

Mix 200 g/7 oz of the flour with all the yeast and enough warm water to make a thick batter, then leave to rise overnight.

Add the rest of the flour, the salt and butter to the dough and slowly add enough water to make a soft, pliable dough. Rest the dough for 1 hour.

Line a baking tray. Bang the air out of the dough and roll into a baguette shape. Put it on the baking tray and leave to prove for 1 hour.

Preheat the oven to 220°C/425°F/ mark 7. Before the dough goes into the oven, using a sharp knife, make slashes along its length. Bake for 30 minutes, then transfer to a wire rack to cool.

This is a traditional French bread, flat and leaf-shaped, very much like the focaccia of Italy. It's eaten with cheese and salads. There are many flavours that go well in this style of bread – try peppers, ham, Cheddar cheese or plain basil – c'est bon!

Onion and Bacon Fougasse

400 g/14 oz strong white flour

20 g/¾ oz yeast

200 ml/7½ fl oz water

1½ teaspoons salt

75 ml/3 fl oz olive oil

1 onion, peeled, finely chopped and fried until translucent

3 rashers of back bacon, finely chopped and fried

Makes 3 loaves

Line three baking trays. Put 200 g/7 oz of the flour with all the yeast and about 175 ml/6 fl oz of water into a bowl and beat together for about 3 minutes into a thick batter. Leave to rise and fall – this should take 3–4 hours.

Add the rest of the flour and water along with the salt, 60 ml/2 fl oz of the oil, the fried onions and bacon and knead well for 5 minutes. Put back in the bowl and leave to rise for 1 hour.

Divide the dough into three pieces. Using a rolling pin, flatten each piece to about 2.5 cm/1 inch high, then shape each roughly into a circle. Using your knife, cut two diagonal slashes down the middle of each circle and three diagonal slashes on each side. Brush lightly with the remaining olive oil, place on the baking trays and leave to rise for 1 hour.

Preheat the oven to 230°C/450°F/mark 8. Bake the bread for 15 minutes until golden brown, then transfer to a wire rack to cool.

Brioche was rumoured to have been first made around the area where Brie is made, so this is a marriage made in heaven. You need to make the dough the day before.

During my time at the Dorchester Hotel in London, this brioche was a great favourite of the Sultan of Brunei. It's fabulous when toasted and served on a bed of rocket salad, with a lemon and dill vinaigrette. You need to make the dough the day before.

Brie and Brioche Parcels *Illustrated*

1 quantity Brioche dough (see page 43)

flour for dusting

250 g/9 oz Brie cheese

1 egg, beaten, for eggwash

Makes 1 brioche

Roll out the brioche dough on a lightly floured surface to about 5 mm/¼ inch thick. Place the cheese in the middle of the dough and fold the sides of the dough neatly onto the middle.

Turn the parcel over and brush the top with some of the eggwash, then place in the fridge for 1 hour.

Preheat the oven to 200°C/400°F/ mark 6. Line a baking tray. Brush the parcel with eggwash again, then, using the back of a knife, score a criss-cross pattern over the parcel. Place on the baking tray and bake for 15 minutes until golden brown. Serve warm.

Salmon Brioche

500 g/1 lb 2 oz strong white flour, plus extra for dusting

1½ teaspoons salt

50 g/2 oz caster sugar

4 medium eggs

20 g/¾ oz yeast

50 ml/2 fl oz milk

250 g/9 oz butter, softened

150 g/5 oz smoked salmon, sliced

Makes 2 brioche

Put the flour into a bowl with the salt, sugar, eggs and yeast and gently rub the mixture together. Add the milk, then use your hands to mix the ingredients together for 5 minutes. Leave the dough in a warm place to rest for 30 minutes.

Slowly add the butter to the dough, kneading for a further 6 minutes, then leave the dough in the fridge overnight. The dough will solidify in the fridge.

Separate the dough into 16 pieces. Lightly cover your hands with flour and roll each piece into a small ball. Push your thumb halfway through the middle of each dough ball and place a slither of salmon inside. Reshape, using a little flour to stop the dough sticking to your hands, and repeat this process until you have 16 mini-brioche.

Lightly grease and line two 450 g/1 lb loaf tins. Place eight of the balls closely together in each tin and leave to prove until they have reached three-quarters of the way up the tins – about 1 hour.

Preheat the oven to 200°C/400°F/ mark 6. Bake the brioche for 15 minutes, then turn out onto a wire rack and leave to cool slightly before serving.

Brioche is a delicate bread and, with the apricots inside, when toasted is a full breakfast in itself. You need to start this the day before.

Apricot Brioche

375 g/13 oz strong white flour

40 g/1½ oz caster sugar

15 g/½ oz yeast

pinch of salt

75 ml/3 fl oz milk

3 medium eggs

185 g/6½ oz butter, softened

150 g/5 oz soft, ready-to-eat dried apricots, diced

Makes 3 brioche

Put the flour, sugar, yeast, salt, milk and eggs in a food mixer and process, using the blade, for about 5 minutes to a smooth dough. If mixing by hand this will take 8 minutes. Add the butter and mix for a further 5 minutes in a mixer or 10 minutes by hand. Tip the dough out into a bowl, cover and leave in the fridge overnight.

Grease three 450 g/1 lb loaf tins. The dough should now be stiff and easily shaped. Divide the dough into 75 g/3 oz pieces and add 1 teaspoon of the apricots into the middle of each piece. Fold the dough over the filling and shape into little balls. Put the balls in the tins in rows of 2 balls, 1 ball, 2 balls, and so on until the tin is full. Each tin should hold no more than 10 pieces. Leave the brioche to rise for 1–2 hours.

Preheat the oven to 200°C/400°F/mark 6. Bake the brioche for 20 minutes until golden brown, then turn out and cool on a wire rack. Cut into slices, toast and serve with lots of butter.

Italian Breads

This recipe is perfect for making pizzas and garlic bread: simply flatten the dough out and use as a pizza base or brush with garlic oil and you have instant garlic bread.

Ciabatta

500 g/1 lb 2 oz strong white flour, plus extra for dusting

1½ teaspoons salt

15 g/½ oz instant yeast

400 ml/14 fl oz tepid water

30 ml/1 fl oz olive oil

Makes 4 loaves

Place the flour, salt, yeast and 300ml of the water in a table mixer with a dough hook and mix on slow for 3 minutes (this will bring the ingredients together).

Then slowly begin to add the remaining water and mix for a further 5–8 minutes on a medium speed. The dough should now be wet and stretch easily when pulled.

Place the dough into an oiled 2 litre square plastic tub and leave it to double in size, this should take about 1 hour in ambient room temperature (20–24°C/68–75°F).

Tip the dough out onto a heavily-floured surface and coat the top of the dough all over with flour. Cut the dough in half lengthways and divide each piece in two so you have four pieces of dough.

Stretch out each piece of dough a little and place on two lined baking trays to rest for a further 20 minutes. Meanwhile preheat the oven to 220°C/425°F/mark 7.

Bake in the oven for 25 minutes until golden brown.

Focaccia are both gorgeous to look at and to eat. They epitomize the Italian philosophy on bread – simple but effective flavourings. You will need to prepare the garlic oil the night before.

Focaccia Pugliese with Tomatoes and Garlic

4 garlic cloves, peeled and crushed

150 ml/¼ pint olive oil

500 g/1 lb 2 oz strong white flour, plus extra for dusting

10 g/¼ oz salt

20 g/¾ oz yeast

300 ml/½ pint water

salt water made from 30 g/1 oz salt dissolved in 100 ml/3½ fl oz warm water

6 plum tomatoes, thinly sliced

Makes 1 loaf

Add the garlic to the olive oil then leave to infuse overnight.

Put the flour, salt, yeast, half the infused olive oil and all the water into a large bowl and mix together for 4 minutes. Tip out onto a lightly floured surface and knead for 6 minutes, then put back in the bowl to rest for 1 hour.

Line a baking tray. Tip the dough out onto your floured surface and roll out a rectangle about 2.5 cm/1 inch thick. Sprinkle with the salt water and the remaining olive oil, then, using a knife, prick the top of the dough all over. Place the tomatoes on top of the dough, then put on the baking tray and leave to rise for 1 hour.

Preheat the oven to 220°C/425°F/mark 7. Bake the bread for 25–30 minutes until golden brown. Eat warm.

I made this with a couple of Sicilian friends when I was in Italy, and was astounded by the flavours from the potatoes – they marry so well with the rosemary and bread.

Potato Focaccia Pugliese

500 g/1 lb 2 oz strong white flour, plus extra for dusting

10 g/¼ oz salt

20 g/¾ oz yeast

300 ml/½ pint water

olive oil

8–10 new potatoes, scrubbed and thinly sliced

rock salt, to sprinkle

2 sprigs fresh rosemary, destalked

Makes 1 loaf

Put the flour, salt, yeast and water into a bowl and mix to form a dough. Leave in the bowl to double in size for about 1 hour.

Line a baking tray. Tip the dough out of the bowl onto the baking tray and flatten with your hands, then brush with olive oil and, using your fingers, make indentations over the surface. Layer the potatoes over the top, sprinkle with a little rock salt and stud with the rosemary sprigs. Leave to rise on the baking tray for 1 hour.

Preheat the oven to 230°C/450°F/mark 8. Bake the bread for 30 minutes. Remove from the oven and brush the loaf with more olive oil, then transfer to a wire rack and serve when cooled.

This focaccia perfectly complements tomato-based pasta dishes and thick winter soups. For extra richness drizzle over a little olive oil and sprinkle with chopped garlic.

Mushroom, Onion and Basil Focaccia

500 g/1 lb 2 oz strong white flour

1½ teaspoons salt

15 g/½ oz yeast

60 ml/2 fl oz olive oil, plus extra for frying and drizzling

water to mix

100 g/3½ oz button mushrooms, chopped

3 onions, peeled and chopped

butter for frying

freshly chopped basil leaves

rock salt, for sprinkling

Makes 1 loaf

Put the flour, salt and yeast into a bowl and mix thoroughly by hand. Add the olive oil, then slowly add sufficient water to make a dough. Mix until the dough comes away from the sides of the bowl. Tip the dough out onto a lightly floured surface and knead well for 5 minutes. When the dough is pliable, put back in the bowl, cover and leave to rest for about 1 hour.

Meanwhile, fry the mushrooms and onions in a little butter and olive oil until browned. Set aside.

Add the mushrooms, onions and a handful of chopped basil to the dough, pressing them into the mixture with your hands.

Grease a 30.5 cm/12 inch loaf tin. Transfer the dough to the tin and press out evenly to the edges. Leave to rest for 30 minutes.

Using your fingers, make indentations all over the dough, brush lightly with olive oil and sprinkle with rock salt. Leave to prove for 1½ hours.

Preheat the oven to 200°C/400°F/mark 6. Bake the bread for 20–30 minutes until golden brown. Eat warm.

Traditional Breads

Authentic naan needs to be baked in a specially made brick oven, but I decided to shallow-fry the dough instead, which gives it this light and fluffy, golden finish. It's excellent as finger food, cut into thin slices and served with a chilled aubergine and crème fraîche dip.

I was asked by a chef to come up with a naan to go with his extensive buffet. I love curries so this was the obvious recipe.

Naan Bread

500 g/1 lb 2 oz strong white flour, plus extra for dusting

1½ teaspoons salt

15 g/½ oz yeast

water to mix

1 teaspoon cumin seeds

1 teaspoon caraway seeds

olive oil for frying

Makes 3 naan

Line a baking tray. Put the flour, salt and yeast into a bowl and add enough water to make a soft, but not sloppy dough. Add the seeds, then divide the dough into three pieces, put on the baking tray and leave to rest for 1 hour.

Turn the dough out onto a lightly floured surface and, using a rolling pin, flatten each piece into a circle, 25.5 cm/ 10 inches in diameter, and leave to rest for 5 minutes.

Heat a frying pan to a medium heat and add a splash of olive oil. Shallow-fry each naan until browned on both sides, then set aside to cool slightly before serving.

Curried Naan Bread *Illustrated*

500 g/1 lb 2 oz strong white flour, plus extra for dusting

1½ teaspoons salt

1 tablespoon olive oil, plus extra for frying

50 g/2 oz mild curry powder

15 g/½ oz yeast

300 ml/½ pint water

100 g/3½ oz sultanas

3 tablespoons mango chutney

Makes 6 naan

Put the flour, salt, oil, curry powder, yeast and water into a bowl and mix together for 2 minutes. Tip out onto a lightly floured surface and knead for 5 minutes until the dough is soft and pliable. Leave to rise for 30 minutes.

Line a baking tray. Incorporate the sultanas and chutney into the dough. Divide the dough into six pieces, put on the baking tray and leave to rest for 1 hour.

Turn the dough out onto a lightly floured surface and, using a rolling pin, flatten each piece into a circle, 25.5 cm/ 10 inches in diameter, put back on the tray and leave to rest for 5 minutes.

Heat a frying pan to a medium heat and add a splash of olive oil. Shallow-fry each dough until browned on both sides, then set aside to cool slightly before serving.

This recipe comes from a tiny village called Kouklia, in the south of Cyprus. Breadmaking is a social occasion for Cypriots and I spent one marvellous afternoon with friends making bread for the whole village. Afterwards we sat and ate the warm loaves with hummus, tzatziki, grilled meats and salad – fantastic!

Cypriot Olive and Coriander Bread

500 g/1 lb 2 oz strong white flour, plus extra for dusting

1½ teaspoons salt

30 ml/1 fl oz olive oil

20 g/¾ oz yeast

300 ml/½ pint warm water

150 g/5 oz black Greek olives, pitted and chopped

75 g/3 oz onion, peeled and chopped

handful of fresh coriander leaves, chopped

Makes 2 loaves

Put the flour into a large bowl and add the salt and oil. Dilute the yeast in a little warm water and add to the mixture. Slowly add the warm water, folding it in with your hand until the dough becomes pliable.

Tip the dough out onto a lightly floured surface and knead for 5 minutes, then put the dough back in the bowl, cover and leave for 1 hour in a warm place.

Line a baking tray. Divide the dough into two pieces and divide half the olives, onions and coriander between each piece. The dough will now be bulging. Mould each dough into a round shape and press firmly down. Sprinkle each lightly with flour and mark a cross in each one, then put them on the baking tray and leave in a warm place for 1 hour.

Preheat the oven to 220°C/425°F/mark 7. Bake the loaves for 30 minutes until golden brown, then transfer to a wire rack to cool.

When I lived in Cyprus, every Sunday I would visit the villages of my friends and invariably make bread. This bread is very common in Cyprus and is best served with dips and a good olive salad. mastika and mechlebe are spices and seeds used in many Greek/Cypriot dishes. They have a similar flavour to fennel or aniseed, which you can use to replace them. However, most good health food shops will stock them.

Koulouri – Cypriot Village Bread

pinch of mastika

pinch of mechlebe

500 g/1 lb 2 oz strong white flour, plus extra for dusting

1½ teaspoons salt

20 g/¾ oz yeast

50 ml/2 fl oz olive oil

300 ml/½ pint water

100 g/3½ oz sesame seeds

1 tablespoon black cumin seeds

1 tablespoon caraway seeds

Makes 1 loaf

Grind the mastika and mechlebe with a pestle and mortar to a smooth powder. Put the flour, salt, yeast, olive oil and water in a large bowl and blend together. Add the mastika and mechlebe powder and knead for 5 minutes, then leave the dough in the bowl to rest for 1 hour.

Tip the seeds into a large bowl and pour a little warm water on them just to dampen them. This will also balloon the sesame seeds and release their juice.

Line a baking tray. Tip the dough out onto a lightly floured surface and shape into a ball. Drop the dough into the dampened seeds and turn until covered in the seeds, then place the dough on the baking tray and leave to rise for 1 hour.

Preheat the oven to 220°C/425°F/mark 7. Using a knife, make a cut around the middle of the ball and two on top. Bake in the oven for 30 minutes until golden brown, then transfer to a wire rack to cool.

This is a traditional Cypriot bread, and is eaten throughout the year in Cyprus.

Halloumi and Mint Bread

500 g/1 lb 2 oz strong
white flour, plus extra
for dusting

10 g/¼ oz salt

60 ml/2 fl oz olive oil

20 g/¾ oz yeast

300 ml/½ pint water

2 packets halloumi
cheese, crumbled

20 g/¾ oz dried mint

Makes 1 loaf

Put the flour, salt, olive oil and yeast into a bowl and slowly add enough water just to bring the ingredients together. Mix for 3 minutes, then tip out onto a lightly floured surface and knead for 5 minutes. (If you are using a food mixer, use the hook and mix for 5 minutes in total.) Put the dough back in the bowl and leave to rise for 1 hour.

Line a baking tray. Add the cheese and dried mint to the dough and shape into a sausage. Taper the ends and place on the baking tray to rest for 1 hour.

Preheat the oven to 220°C/425°F/mark 7. Cut diagonal slashes across the top of the dough and dust with flour. Bake for 25–30 minutes until golden brown, then transfer to a wire rack to cool.

A traditional bread made in Cyprus around Green Monday, the day the fasting starts before Easter. The bread is usually eaten with fresh vegetables and fruit.

Try using ground fennel if mastika is difficult to get hold of, but any good health food shop should stock it.

Laganes Bread

1 teaspoon mastika

500 g/1 lb 2 oz strong white flour, plus extra for dusting

10 g/¼ oz salt

20 g/¾ oz yeast

60 ml/2 fl oz olive oil

300 ml/½ pint water

100 g/3½ oz sesame seeds

1 tablespoon caraway seeds

1½ tablespoons black cumin seeds

Makes 2 loaves

Grind the mastika with a mortar and pestle to a smooth powder. Put the flour, salt, yeast, olive oil and water into a bowl and mix together for 3 minutes. Add the mastika powder to the dough, then tip the dough out onto a lightly floured surface. Using your fingers and the heel of your palm, knead for 5 minutes, then put the dough back in the bowl and leave to rise for 1 hour.

Meanwhile, put the sesame, caraway and black cumin seeds into a bowl and pour over just enough warm water to cover. Leave for 20 minutes – this balloons the seeds and releases their flavours.

Line a baking tray. Tip the dough out onto your floured surface and divide into two pieces. Flatten each piece into an oval shape, 2.5–5 cm/1–2 inches thick, and turn them in the seed mixture until the dough is completely covered, top and bottom. Put onto the baking tray and leave to rise for 1 hour.

Preheat the oven to 220°C/425°F/mark 7. Using your finger, press holes over the top of the dough, then bake the loaves for 25 minutes until golden brown. Transfer to a wire rack to cool.

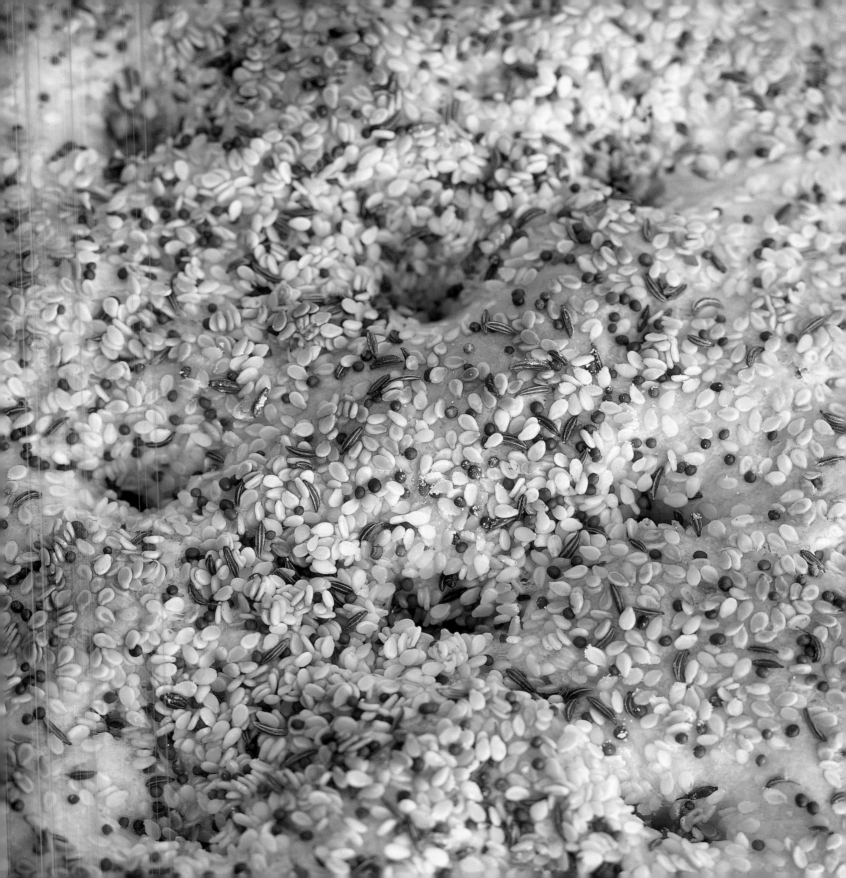

I have kept this bread as authentic as possible. You will find the mastika and mechlebe in any good health shop, but you can use ground fennel as an alternative. I've made this bread several times on television and it remains a firm favourite.

Tsoureki – Cypriot Easter Bread

500 g/1 lb 2 oz strong white flour, plus extra for dusting

60 g/2½ oz butter, softened

75 g/3 oz caster sugar

pinch of cinnamon

pinch of mastika

pinch of mechlebe

handful of sultanas

150 ml/5 fl oz milk

zest of 1 orange

10 g/¼ oz salt

15 g/½ oz yeast

150 ml/5 fl oz warm water

3 eggs, hardboiled in their shells with red food colouring

1 egg, beaten, for eggwash

Makes 1 loaf

Put the flour into a large bowl, add all the other ingredients except the yeast, water and eggs and mix together briefly. Dilute the yeast in a little warm water and add to the mixture. Slowly add the remaining warm water, mixing it in as you do, until you have a soft dough consistency.

Tip the dough out onto a lightly floured surface and knead until you have a pliable dough. Put the dough back in the bowl and leave to rest for 1 hour.

Line a baking tray. Divide the dough into two and roll into strips. Plait the strips together, put on the baking tray and leave to rise in a warm place for 1 hour.

Preheat the oven to 200°C/400°F/mark 6. Brush the top of the bread with eggwash and place the coloured eggs along the top of the bread. Bake for 25 minutes, then transfer to a wire rack to cool.

The ancient Egyptians used to bake their bread in cone-shaped terracotta pots and this is the updated version, although the herbs and onions are authentic ingredients. This bread is particularly good for dinner parties – the little pots are very eye-catching and you could even try painting them for extra effect.

Pepper and Onion Flowerpot Bread

1½ teaspoons salt

50 g/2 oz butter, softened

500 g/1 lb 2 oz strong white flour

20 g/¾ oz yeast

warm water to mix

2 large onions, peeled and finely chopped

olive oil for frying

30 g/1 oz fresh basil leaves, roughly chopped

3 red peppers, deseeded and finely chopped

Makes 3 loaves

You will need three flowerpots for this recipe, each 10 cm/4 inches in diameter and 25.5 cm/10 inches high.

Add the salt and butter to the flour and rub together. Dilute the yeast in a little water and add this to the flour, then mix in enough warm water to make the dough pliable. Knead the dough well for 5 minutes, until elasticated. Place in a bowl, cover and leave in a warm place to rest for 1 hour.

Fry the onions in a little olive oil until translucent, then set aside to cool. When cool, mix with the basil and peppers, add to the dough and blend together. Divide the dough into three equal pieces and mould them into rounds.

Line the insides and bottoms of the flowerpots with silicone paper. Place a ball of dough inside each pot and leave to prove for 1 hour.

Preheat the oven to 200°C/400°F/mark 6. Bake the flowerpots for 30 minutes. Turn the breads out onto a wire rack to cool, then return them to the unlined flowerpots for display on your dining table.

Herb and Seed Breads

This is an aromatic bread, full of flavour. Basil is a favourite herb of mine, and mixed with the coriander it's perfect. This bread is great as the base for cheese on toast.

Herb Bread

500 g/1 lb 2 oz strong white flour, plus extra for dusting

10 g/¼ oz salt

20 g/¾ oz yeast

75 ml/3 fl oz olive oil

300 ml/½ pint water

1 packet fresh basil

1 packet fresh coriander

1 packet fresh dill

Makes 2 loaves

Put the flour, salt, yeast, olive oil and water into a bowl and, using your hands, mix together for 3 minutes. When the dough has formed, tip out onto a lightly floured surface and, using your fingers and heel of your palm, knead for 6 minutes. Put the dough back in the bowl and leave to rise for 1 hour.

Preheat the oven to 220°C/425°F/mark 7. Line a baking tray. Destalk all the herbs, then rip them up roughly and mix into the dough. Divide the dough into two pieces and shape each into a ball. Flatten slightly with your hands and cut two slashes across the top of each one. Place on the baking tray and bake for 30 minutes. Transfer to a wire rack to cool.

You can also try making this recipe with Philadelphia cream cheese instead of the ricotta, for a creamy bread with tight airholes. Either way served toasted with cheese it is unbeatable.

Ricotta and Chive Loaf

500 g/1 lb 2 oz strong white flour, plus extra for sprinkling

1½ teaspoons salt

20 g/¾ oz yeast

75 ml/3 fl oz olive oil

300 ml/½ pint water

125 g/4 oz ricotta cheese

2 tablespoons snipped chives

Makes 1 loaf

Put the flour, salt, yeast, olive oil, water and cheese into a large bowl and mix with your hands for 3 minutes. Tip out onto a lightly floured surface and knead for 2 minutes, then add the chives and knead for 3 minutes more. Put the dough back in the bowl and leave to rest for 1 hour.

Line a baking tray. Tip the dough out onto a lightly floured surface and shape into a sausage shape, tapered at each end. Place the bread on the baking tray and leave to rise for 1 hour.

Preheat the oven to 220°C/425°F/mark 7. Bake the bread for 25 minutes, then transfer to a wire rack to cool.

This bread is definitely a meal on its own – serve it as a sandwich, sliced thinly, filled with roast garlic lamb and salad leaves with a lemon dressing. It also makes a great accompaniment to a thick soup topped with cheese. You need to start this bread the day before.

Potato and Dill Bread

20 g/¾ oz yeast

water to mix

500 g/1 lb 2 oz strong white flour

1½ teaspoons salt

8 medium new potatoes, scrubbed

1 garlic clove, peeled and chopped

butter and olive oil, for frying

30 g/1 oz fresh dill, destalked and chopped

Makes 2 loaves

Dilute the yeast in a little warm water. Put the flour and salt into a bowl, and add the diluted yeast. Slowly add enough water to the flour until you have a malleable dough, then leave to rest overnight.

Boil the potatoes for 5 minutes, leave to cool, then cut into quarters. Fry the potatoes and garlic in a little butter and oil until golden brown, then leave them to cool.

Grease a baking tray. Divide your dough into two pieces and flatten them into an oval shape. Place on the baking tray and leave to rise for 1–2 hours.

Preheat the oven to 230°C/450°F/mark 8. Cover the two pieces of dough equally with the potato mixture, pressing it in firmly. Sprinkle some dill over the top and bake in the oven for 25–30 minutes until golden brown. Transfer to a wire rack to cool.

I was asked to make a bread for Spyros, a friend in Cyprus; he loved sunflower seeds so I came up with this. I hope you like it. It will last longer if the butter is omitted, but it gives it a richer flavour.

This loaf you love or you hate, mainly because of the caraway seeds. You need to start this the night before.

Sunflower Seed Bread *Illustrated*

250 g/9 oz wholemeal flour

250 g/9 oz strong white flour, plus extra for dusting

10 g/¼ oz salt

20 g/¾ oz yeast

50 g/2 oz butter (optional)

300 ml/½ pint water

150 g/5 oz sunflower seeds

Makes 1 loaf

Put the flours, salt, yeast, butter (if using) and water into a large bowl and mix to a soft pliable dough (add a little extra water if necessary). Tip out onto a lightly floured surface and knead for 5–6 minutes until you have a very smooth dough, then put the dough back in the bowl and leave to rest for 1 hour.

Line a baking tray. Incorporate the sunflower seeds into the dough, then shape the dough into a ball and flatten with your hands. Using a knife, make vertical slashes around the sides of the dough, from top to bottom, then roll the dough in any remaining seeds. Put onto the baking tray and leave to rise in a warm place for 1 hour.

Preheat the oven to 220°C/425°F/ mark 7. Bake the loaf for 30 minutes until golden brown, then transfer to a wire rack to cool.

Rye with Caraway

300 g/11 oz rye flour, plus extra for dusting

200 g/7 oz strong white flour, plus extra for dusting

20 g/¾ oz yeast

300 ml/½ pint water

1½ teaspoons salt

60 g/2½ oz butter, softened

60 g/2½ oz caraway seeds

Makes 1 loaf

Put half the rye flour, half the white flour and all the yeast into a large bowl, then add about 175 ml/6 fl oz of water and mix well until you have a thick paste. Leave this dough in the bowl overnight for 10–12 hours.

Add the rest of the flours, the salt, butter, caraway seeds and remaining water and mix well in the bowl for 3 minutes. Tip out onto a lightly floured surface and knead well for 3 minutes, then put the dough back in the bowl and leave to rise for 1 hour.

Line a baking tray. Tip the dough out onto your floured surface and roll into a ball, then, using a rolling pin, flatten it slightly into a disc. Cover the top with rye flour, put the dough on the baking tray and leave to rise for 2 hours.

Preheat the oven to 220°C/425°F/ mark 7. Bake the loaf for 30 minutes, then serve warm with smoked salmon.

Fruit and Nut Breads

This bread was one of the first breads I made when I worked at the Chester Grosvenor Hotel. It was produced for the restaurant and went well with the cheeseboard. It's a real old favourite.

You can also make this bread with 100 per cent white flour. This will give a slightly different texture.

Stilton and Walnut Wholemeal Loaf

100 g/3½ oz strong white flour, plus extra for dusting

400 g/14 oz wholemeal flour

10 g/¼ oz salt

20 g/¾ oz yeast

50 g/2 oz butter, softened

300 ml/½ pint water

100 g/3½ oz Stilton cheese, crumbled

125 g/4 oz walnuts, chopped

Makes 1 loaf

Put the flours, salt, yeast and butter into a bowl. Add the water, a little at a time, and gradually incorporate all the flour from the sides of the bowl.

Turn the dough out onto a lightly floured surface and knead for 5 minutes until the dough is smooth and pliable. Put back in the bowl and leave to rise for 1 hour.

Line a baking tray. Add the Stilton and walnuts to the dough and mix well together. Divide the dough into three pieces and roll each one into a long sausage. Plait the dough – place the three strips side by side and join them at the top, then bring the right strip over the middle strip, then the left strip over, and continue until the plait is complete. Put on the tray and leave to rise for 1 hour.

Preheat the oven to 230°C/450°F/mark 8. Bake the loaf for 30 minutes then transfer to a wire rack to cool.

Made on Good Friday, this bread is eaten throughout the Easter weekend, so you can throw the chocolates away.

This is a moist, chewy bread packed with goodness. For me it's a breakfast bread, but it would be equally at home on a cheeseboard.

Fruit Bread

500 g/1 lb 2 oz strong white flour, plus extra for dusting

10 g/¼ oz salt

20 g/¾ oz yeast

75 g/3 oz caster sugar

75 g/3 oz butter, softened

3 medium eggs, beaten

300 ml/½ pint milk and water mixed

1 tablespoon ground cinnamon

50 g/2 oz mandarin segments

75 g/3 oz sultanas

60 g/2½ oz mixed peel

zest of 3 lemons

zest of 3 oranges

Makes 2 loaves

Put the flour, salt, yeast, sugar, butter and eggs into a large bowl. Gradually add the milk and water mixture and bind the ingredients together for 3 minutes. Tip the dough out onto a lightly floured surface and knead for 5 minutes, then put the dough back in the bowl and leave for 1½ hours to rise.

Line a baking tray. Incorporate the cinnamon, mandarins, sultanas, mixed peel and zests into the dough, then divide the dough into two pieces and shape each into a ball. Flatten the balls to about 7.5 cm/3 inches thick, then, using a knife, score each piece into eight equal segments. Place the dough on the baking tray and leave to rise for 1 hour.

Preheat the oven to 220°C/425°F/ mark 7. Bake the breads for 20 minutes until golden brown, then transfer to a wire rack to cool.

Date and Fig Bread *Illustrated*

400 g/14 oz wholemeal flour

100 g/3½ oz strong white flour, plus extra for dusting

10 g/¼ oz salt

20 g/¾ oz yeast

50 g/2 oz butter, softened

1 tablespoon treacle

300 ml/½ pint water

75 g/3 oz dried figs, chopped

75 g/3 oz dates, chopped

Makes 2 small loaves

Put the flours, salt, yeast, butter, treacle and water into a bowl and mix for 5 minutes. Tip out onto a lightly floured surface and knead for 5 minutes, then put the dough back in the bowl and leave for 1 hour to rise.

Line a baking tray. Incorporate the figs and dates into the dough, then divide it into two pieces. Shape the pieces into balls, place on the baking tray and leave to rise for 1 hour.

Preheat the oven to 220°C/425°F/ mark 7. Dust the loaves with flour and, using a knife, make three equidistant horizontal cuts all around each ball. Bake for 30 minutes, then transfer to a wire rack to cool.

This bread was inspired by a friend of mine, Chris Davies, an avid cook who wanted an unusual bread for his dinner guests. I think it did the trick!

John Woods, the Executive Chef at the Cliveden hotel, asked me to make a bread to complement his new cheeseboard, so after various experiments I came up with this one. Its sweet, slightly nutty flavour is delicious with Stilton and the stronger French cheeses – try it as a starter topped with baked Camembert and cranberries.

Grape and Sultana Bread

500 g/1 lb 2 oz strong white flour, plus extra for dusting

1½ teaspoons salt

30 g/1 oz caster sugar

20 g/¾ oz yeast, crumbled

30 g/1 oz butter, softened

300 ml/½ pint water

75 g/3 oz red seedless grapes

75 g/3 oz sultanas

Makes 1 loaf

Put the flour, salt, sugar, yeast and butter into a large bowl and mix together, then slowly add the water until all the flour has been incorporated (you might not need all of it). Tip out onto a lightly floured surface and, using your fingers and palms, knead for 5 minutes. Put the bread back in the bowl and leave to rest for 1 hour.

Line a baking tray. Add the grapes and sultanas to the dough and mix in well, then shape into a ball, flatten slightly using your hand and dust the top with flour. Put onto the baking tray and leave to rise for 1 hour.

Preheat the oven to 200°C/400°F/ mark 6. Cut a square in the top of the dough and bake for 25 minutes. Transfer to a wire rack to cool.

Date, Prune and Pecan Bread *Illustrated*

15 g/½ oz yeast

500 g/1 lb 2 oz wholemeal flour, plus extra for dusting

10 g/¼ oz salt

50 g/2 oz butter, softened

water to mix

125 g/4 oz pecans, chopped

150 g/5 oz dates, chopped

40 g/1½ oz soft, ready-to-eat dried prunes, chopped

Makes 2 x 450 g/ 1lb loaves

Dilute the yeast in a little warm water, then put with the flour, salt and butter into a bowl and mix well. Slowly add enough water, mixing all the time, until the dough becomes elastic. Tip out onto a lightly floured surface and knead the dough for 5 minutes. Put the dough back in the bowl and leave to rest for 2 hours.

Divide the dough into two pieces and incorporate half the pecans, dates and prunes into each piece, pressing in firmly. Knead for a further 5 minutes, then rest the loaves for 1 hour.

Preheat the oven to 200°C/400°F/ mark 6. Grease two 450 g/1 lb loaf tins. Flatten each loaf and roll into a sausage shape. Place the seam underneath, then taper each end. Put each loaf into a tin, seam-side down, dust with flour and, using a knife, cut a zigzag pattern on the top. Bake for 25–30 minutes, then turn out onto a wire rack to cool.

An incredibly luxurious bread that will be eaten in one sitting. IF there is any left, use it to make extra-rich bread and butter pudding. This is definitely not a bread to count calories with!

Chocolate and Sour Cherry Bread

500 g/1 lb 2 oz strong white flour, plus extra for dusting

2 teaspoons salt

30 ml/1 fl oz olive oil

15 g/½ oz yeast

warm water to mix

160 g tin black cherries, drained

200 g packet chocolate chips

Makes 2 loaves

Put the flour into a bowl with the salt, olive oil and yeast. Slowly add the warm water and mix by hand until the dough is pliable.

Tip the dough out onto a lightly floured surface and knead for 4–7 minutes. Put the dough back in the bowl and leave to rest for 1 hour.

Line a baking tray. Divide the dough into two pieces and add half the cherries to each one. (You may need to add a little more flour if the mix becomes too sloppy.) Now add half the chocolate chips to each dough. Mix well, adding a little flour if the dough becomes too soft. Shape the dough into 2 balls and flatten to about 5 cm/2 inches high. Dust heavily with flour and score diagonal lines across the top to form diamond shapes. Place on the baking tray and leave the dough to rest for 1 hour.

Preheat the oven to 200°C/400°F/mark 6. Bake the bread for 20–25 minutes, then transfer to a wire rack to cool.

This is comfort food at its best – rich and filling. Eat it toasted for
tea, dripping with butter or, better still, piled high with baked apples
or peaches with a dollop of fresh vanilla ice cream on top.

Banana and Muesli Bread

**500 g/1 lb 2 oz
wholemeal flour**

2 teaspoons salt

15 g/½ oz yeast

**50 g/2 oz butter,
softened**

320 ml/11 fl oz water

**2 large bananas,
chopped**

1 bowl of muesli

Makes 2 loaves

Put the flour, salt, yeast and butter into a bowl. Slowly add water to the
bowl and mix carefully by hand until the dough becomes elastic. Knead
the dough for 5 minutes, then cover the bowl and set aside to rest for
2 hours.

Divide the dough into two, then add a chopped banana to each, using
your hands to 'mash' the banana into the mixture. Your dough will now
be sticky, so add enough muesli to each to regain the original texture.

Line a baking tray. Roll each dough into a ball, then press into the bowl
of muesli, so that the dough becomes completely coated. Place the
loaves on the baking tray and leave to rise for 1–2 hours.

Preheat the oven to 200°C/400°F/mark 6. Using a knife, deeply score
the top of each ball into 8 sections. Bake the loaves for 25–30 minutes,
then transfer to a wire rack to cool.

This bread is always a great favourite with the kids at teatime, loaded with honey or chocolate spread. For a change, serve it with cream cheese and celery as an energy-giving sandwich.

Peanut Bread

500 g/1 lb 2 oz strong
white flour

1½ teaspoons salt

15 g/½ oz yeast

warm water to mix

¾ jar of crunchy
peanut butter

100 g/3½ oz
caramelized peanut
chips, to mix

Makes 2 loaves

Put the flour, salt and yeast into a bowl. Slowly add warm water and mix by hand until the dough is pliable. Leave in the bowl to rest for 1 hour.

Add the peanut butter to the dough and mix it in thoroughly. The dough will now be sticky, so begin to add the peanut chips until the dough tightens up again. Divide the dough into two pieces and leave to rest for 1 hour.

Grease a baking tray. Punch any air out of the dough pieces and mould into two sausage shapes, approx. 30.5 cm/12 inches long and tapering at each end. Roll them up into a coil, place them on the baking tray and leave to prove for 1 hour.

Preheat the oven to 200°C/400°F/mark 6. Using a sharp knife, score a line down the middle of each loaf and dust each lightly with flour. Bake the loaves for 20–25 minutes, then transfer to a wire rack to cool.

A bread I devised while I was in Cyprus; it's gorgeous toasted and with lashings of butter.

Almond Bread

500 g/1 lb 2 oz strong white flour

10 g/¼ oz salt

60 g/2½ oz caster sugar

40 g/1½ oz butter, softened

75 g/3 oz ground almonds

20 g/¾ oz yeast

300 ml/½ pint milk and water mixed

125 g/4 oz flaked almonds

Makes 1 loaf

Put the flour, salt, sugar, butter, ground almonds and yeast into a bowl. Add the milk and water mix and blend for 2 minutes. Tip out of the bowl onto a lightly floured surface and knead with your hands until the dough becomes soft and pliable. This should take no more than 5 minutes. Put the dough back in the bowl and leave to rise for 1 hour.

Line a baking tray. Tip the dough out onto your floured surface and mix in half the flaked almonds. Flatten the dough into an oval shape and cover the outside of the dough with the remaining flaked almonds. Place the dough on the baking tray and leave to rise for 1 hour.

Preheat the oven to 220°C/425°F/mark 7. Bake the bread for 20–25 minutes, then transfer to a wire rack to cool.

My wife's favourite Danish. Remember Valentine's Day – get baking.
Probably you won't use all the pastries at once, so you can freeze
the finished dough for up to 3 months. You need to start this the
day before.

Apple and Sultana Danish Pastries

For the pastry

20 g/¾ oz yeast

625 g/1 lb 7 oz strong white flour, plus extra for dusting

1½ teaspoons salt

75 g/3 oz caster sugar

water to mix

500 g/1 lb 2 oz butter, chilled

For the filling

10 apples, peeled and cored

100 g/3½ oz sultanas

2 teaspoons ground cinnamon

2 eggs, beaten, for eggwash

apricot jam, warmed, to glaze

For the water icing

lemon zest, icing sugar and water

Makes about 30 Danish pastries

Dilute the yeast in a little warm water and put with the flour, salt and sugar into a large mixing bowl. Using a wooden spoon, slowly mix in a little water until the dough becomes pliable. Tip the dough out onto a lightly floured surface and knead well until it feels elastic. Put the dough back in the bowl and leave in the fridge for 1 hour.

Return the chilled dough to your floured work surface and roll it into a rectangle 60 x 30.5 cm/24 x12 inches. Flatten the chilled butter into a rectangle about 1 cm/½ inch thick and lay it over two-thirds of the dough. Bring the uncovered third of the dough into the centre, then fold the covered top third down, so that your dough is now in three layers. Return the dough to the fridge to chill for 1 hour.

Scatter some more flour over your table and roll out the dough to the same-sized rectangle as before. Repeat the folding process, one side on top of the other, and place the dough back in the fridge for 1 hour. You will need to repeat this process twice more before leaving the dough to rest, wrapped in clingfilm, overnight.

Line a baking tray. Roll out the dough to about 5 mm/¼ inch thick, then cut 12.5 cm/5 inch squares from the dough. Fold the edges into the middle so you have a parcel, place each one onto the baking tray and leave to rise for 2 hours at an ambient temperature (20°C+).

Meanwhile, cook the apples in a pan with a little water to soften them for 7 minutes, then add the sultanas and cinnamon and allow to cool.

Spoon at least 2 tablespoons of the apple mixture into the middle of each dough square. Preheat the oven to 200°C/400°F/mark 6. Brush the eggwash onto the exposed parts of the dough, and bake for 20 minutes. Take out of the oven and brush with warmed apricot jam. Cool, then top with water icing (see page 124).

Once you've prepared the dough and cut out the shapes you can freeze them for use later, if you wish.

This was a favourite of mine at the Cliveden hotel in the morning, eaten with a cup of tea, while sitting by the window looking at the view across the grounds.

Strawberry Danish

Pain au Raisin Danish Pastries *Illustrated*

1 quantity Danish Pastry dough (see page 121)

For the filling

1 punnet of strawberries, quartered

270 ml/9 fl oz extra-thick strawberry yoghurt

1 tin thick custard

1 egg, beaten, for eggwash

1 packet flaked almonds

2 dessertspoons apricot jam

Makes 30–40 Danish pastries

Make the pastry as on page 121, up to the point where it is chilled overnight. Roll out to 3 mm/⅛ inch thick and cut into 30.5 cm/12 inch long by 12.5 cm/5 inch wide pieces. If you find that you don't have enough for these lengths don't worry, make the lengths 20.5 or 15 cm/8 or 6 inches long.

Line several baking trays. Add the strawberries to the yoghurt and fold in the custard. Spoon some of this mixture down the middle of each of the long rectangles and fold in half lengthways. Using a knife, cut lines into the dough widthways about 10 cm/4 inches apart all the way along. Brush with the eggwash and sprinkle the flaked almonds all over the tops. Put the dough on the baking trays and leave to rise for 1 hour.

Preheat the oven to 200°C/400°F/mark 6. Bake the Danish for 20 minutes until golden brown. Transfer to a wire rack to cool, then cut into fingers along the width.

Put the apricot jam in a small saucepan with a splash of water and bring up to boil. Brush this onto the Danish pastries and serve.

1 quantity Danish Pastry dough (see page 121)

For the filling

100 g/3½ oz fresh custard

250 g/9 oz raisins or sultanas

1½ teaspoons cinnamon

1 egg, beaten, for eggwash

100 g/3½ oz apricot jam

For the water icing

lemon zest, icing sugar and water

Makes 40–50 Danish pastries

Make the pastry as on page 121, up to the point where it is chilled overnight.

Using a rolling pin, flatten the dough into a rectangle 3 mm/⅛ inch thick. Spread the custard over the top and sprinkle liberally with raisins or sultanas, add a sprinkle of cinnamon and roll the dough up into a sausage. Line several baking trays. Cut the sausage into 2.5 cm/1 inch pieces, place flat-side down on the baking trays and leave to rise for 1½ hours.

Preheat the oven to 200°C/400°F/mark 6. Brush the Danish lightly with the eggwash and bake for 10–15 minutes until golden brown. Transfer to a wire rack and brush with warm apricot jam. Leave to cool, then top with water icing (see page 124).

This bread reminds me of a little bakery near to where I was brought up in Merseyside. On my way back from school I would buy a Sally Lunn and eat it with butter when I got home.

Sally Lunns

400 g/14 oz strong white flour, plus extra for dusting

1½ teaspoons salt

40 g/1½ oz caster sugar

40 g/1½ oz butter, softened

20 g/¾ oz yeast

120 ml/4 fl oz milk

120 ml/4 fl oz water, plus extra for icing

50 g/2 oz sultanas

60 g/2½ oz glacé cherries

1 teaspoon ground cinnamon

zest of 3 oranges

75 g/3 oz icing sugar

Makes 1 loaf

Put the flour, salt, sugar, butter, yeast, milk and water into a bowl and mix together with your hands. When all the flour has been incorporated tip the dough out onto a lightly floured surface and knead until smooth and pliable. Put the dough back in the bowl and leave for 1 hour to rest.

Line a baking tray. Add the sultanas, cherries, cinnamon and orange zest to the dough and, using an electric mixer (blade attachment) or your hands, work it in well. Shape the dough into a sausage shape by flattening out the dough and rolling it up. Place the dough on the baking tray and leave to rise for 1 hour.

Preheat the oven to 200°C/400°F/mark 6. Bake the dough for 20 minutes, then transfer to a wire rack to cool.

While it is cooling, make a water icing. Tip the icing sugar into a bowl, add a little water and mix in well, then gradually add water until the icing coats the back of a spoon. Drizzle the icing over the top of the bread. Cut into slices and eat with lashings of butter.

These are great toasted, with butter.

Teacakes

400 g/14 oz strong white flour, plus extra for dusting

1½ teaspoons salt

40 g/1½ oz caster sugar

1 teaspoon ground cinnamon

50 g/2 oz butter, softened

20 g/¾ oz yeast

200 ml/7½ fl oz water

75 g/3 oz sultanas

60 g/2½ oz mixed peel

1 egg, beaten, for eggwash

Makes 10–15

Put the flour, salt, sugar, cinnamon, butter, yeast and water into a large bowl and mix together for 2 minutes. Tip the dough out onto a lightly floured surface and knead for 5 minutes, then put back into the bowl and leave for 1 hour to rest.

Line a baking tray. Add the sultanas and mixed peel to the dough and divide the dough into 75 g/3 oz pieces. Shape each piece into a ball and, using a rolling pin, flatten them out to 2.5 cm/1 inch thick. Place the teacakes on the baking tray and leave to rise for 1 hour.

Preheat the oven to 190°C/375°F/mark 5. Brush the teacakes with eggwash and bake for 15 minutes.

I wanted to go back to the way we used to make Hot Cross Buns,
using real fruit rather than all dried. The result is this juicy bun – the
kids will love it, and adults will too!

Hollywood Hot Cross Buns

500 g/1 lb 2 oz strong
white flour, plus extra
for dusting

1½ teaspoons salt

75 g/3 oz caster sugar

25 g/1 oz yeast

300 ml/½ pint milk
and water mixed

60 g/2½ oz mandarin
segments, chopped

60 g/2½ oz peach
slices, chopped

60 g/2½ oz apple
slices, chopped

2 teaspoons ground
cinnamon

60 g/2½ oz apricot
jam, warmed, to glaze

For the crosses
200 ml/7 fl oz water
200 g/7 oz flour
2 medium eggs
Makes 15–20

Put the flour, salt, sugar and yeast into a bowl. Slowly add enough of
the milk and water mix to achieve a pliable dough. Tip out onto a lightly
floured surface and knead well for 5 minutes, then put the dough back
in the bowl and leave to rise for 1 hour.

Incorporate the mandarins, peaches, apples and cinnamon into the
dough and leave to rise for 1 hour.

Line a baking tray. Divide the dough into 75 g/3 oz pieces and roll each
into a ball. Put them on the baking tray and leave to rest for 1 hour.

Preheat the oven to 200°C/400°F/mark 6. To make the crosses, whisk
together the water, flour and eggs to a smooth paste and pipe a cross on
top of each bun. Bake the buns for 25 minutes until golden brown.
Take out of the oven and brush them with warmed apricot jam. Serve
immediately.

An obvious treat for my son Joshua, and a favourite of mine when I'm watching a video on those cold winter days.

Doughnuts

250 g/9 oz strong white flour, plus extra for dusting

pinch of salt

40 g/1½ oz caster sugar

30 g/1 oz butter, softened

150 ml/¼ pint water

20 g/¾ oz yeast

vegetable or sunflower oil for frying

caster sugar, to coat

Makes 5–10

Put all the ingredients except the oil and coating sugar into a large bowl and mix together, then tip out onto a lightly floured surface and knead for 5 minutes. Put the dough back in the bowl and leave to double in size.

Divide the dough into 75 g/3 oz pieces and shape into balls. Put on your floured surface and leave to rise until doubled in size.

Pour some vegetable or sunflower oil into a large heavy-based pan and heat to 170°C/325°F, or a medium heat. Lower each of the doughnuts into the oil and fry until brown, then roll them over and fry the other side. (If you have a problem with rolling the doughnuts over then pierce them slightly with a knife.) The frying should take no more than 5 minutes for both sides. When they are browned, tip them straight into a bowl full of caster sugar and coat well. Cool them on a wire rack, then enjoy with a nice cup of tea.

Sweet Treats

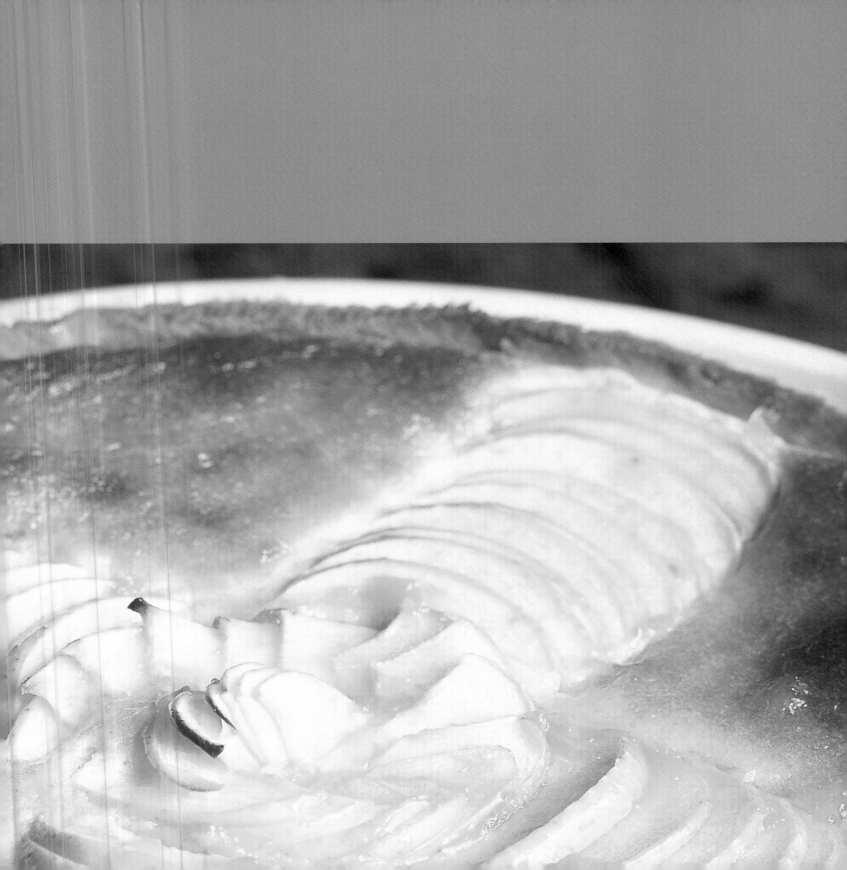

This has to be the easiest ice cream to make and it is absolutely delicious. Serve it stuffed into baked pears or peaches or as a sweet pancake filling – unbelievable!

This has the edge over traditional bread and butter pudding – the buttery croissants and tartness of the blueberries really lifts this dish.

Brown Bread Ice Cream

75 g/3 oz brown breadcrumbs (from Guinness and Treacle Bread, page 28)

60 g/2½ oz brown sugar

3 large eggs, separated

1 tablespoon dark rum

270 ml/9 fl oz double cream

75 g/3 oz icing sugar

Serves 4–6

Mix the breadcrumbs and brown sugar together, then place on a baking tray and grill for 8 minutes or until dark and caramelized. When the mixture is cool, break up into small, bite-sized pieces.

Whisk the egg whites until stiff. In a separate bowl, mix the egg yolks with the rum, then fold this mixture into the egg whites. Finally, whisk the cream and icing sugar together, then, using a metal spoon, fold the cream and breadcrumbs into the egg mixture. Pour into a metal container and freeze for about 4 hours before serving.

Croissant Pudding

12 butter croissants (see page 48)

75 g/3 oz blackberries, plus a few extra to serve

75 g/3 oz blueberries, plus a few extra to serve

75 g/3 oz raspberries, plus a few extra to serve

splash of kirsch

icing sugar

For the sauce Anglaise

400 ml/14 fl oz milk

2 vanilla pods

3 medium eggs

40 g/1½ oz caster sugar

Serves 6

Preheat the oven to 180°C/350°F/ mark 4. Cut the croissants lengthways and place in a large casserole dish. Sprinkle over the berries and add a splash of kirsch.

To make the sauce Anglaise, put the milk and vanilla pods in a pan and bring to the boil. Whisk the eggs and sugar together to a froth, then pour the milk onto the eggs and return to the pan. Boil for 6 minutes to reduce, then pour over the croissants in the casserole dish.

Bake in the oven for 30 minutes. Take out of the oven, sprinkle with icing sugar and caramelize with a blow torch or under the grill. Serve with pouring cream and more berries.

I made this recipe for Easter some years back. It appeals to both children and adults alike.

Savarin with Chocolate Sauce and Eggs

For the savarin

450 g/1 lb strong white flour

175 ml/6 fl oz milk

50 g/2 oz yeast

pinch of salt

60 g/2½ oz caster sugar

4 medium eggs

200 g/7 oz butter

For the sauce

1 bar milk chocolate, melted

1 carton thick custard

To decorate

apricot jam, warmed, or warm stock syrup (½ sugar to ½ water)

mini chocolate eggs

Serves 8

To make the savarin, put all the ingredients into a bowl and mix together. Beat well for 6 minutes until smooth, then place in a savarin ring and leave to rise for 1 hour until light to touch.

Preheat the oven to 200°C/400°F/mark 6. Bake the savarin for 25 minutes until golden brown.

Meanwhile, make the chocolate sauce by stirring the melted chocolate into the custard.

Tip the savarin out of the ring and brush with the warm apricot jam or stock syrup, if using. Fill the centre with chocolate sauce and top with mini eggs.

These muffins are great eaten warm and covered with pouring cream, or serve them cold as a snack. Either way they're a winner.

Blueberry Muffins *Illustrated*

250 g/9 oz butter, softened	Preheat the oven to 200°C/400°F/ mark 6. Cream the butter and sugar until white and fluffy, then add the eggs and mix for a further 5 minutes. Sift in the flour and baking powder and mix into a smooth paste.
185 g/6½ oz caster sugar	
4 medium eggs	
250 g/9 oz strong white flour	
1½ teaspoons baking powder	Line your muffin tray with the paper cases and drop a spoonful of the mixture into each case. Gently press the blueberries into the centre of each muffin.
16 paper muffin cases	
2 punnets blueberries	
icing sugar, for dusting	
Makes 16 muffins	Bake for 12 minutes or until a muffin springs back when pressed. Transfer to a wire rack to cool, then dust lightly with icing sugar.

These muffins are just spectacular served at teatime with a dollop of clotted cream, preferably accompanying cucumber sandwiches and a cup of Earl Grey tea – anyone for tennis?

Wimbledon Muffins

250 g/9 oz butter, softened	Preheat the oven to 200°C/400°F/ mark 6. Cream the butter and sugar until white and fluffy, then add the eggs and mix for a further 5 minutes. Sift in the flour and baking powder and mix into a smooth paste.
185 g/6½ oz caster sugar	
5 medium eggs	
250 g/9 oz strong white flour	
1½ teaspoons baking powder	Line your muffin tray with the paper cases and drop a spoonful of the mixture into each one. Gently press the sliced strawberries into the centre of each muffin.
16 paper muffin cases	
16 medium-size strawberries, each sliced into 3	
icing sugar, for dusting	
Makes 16 muffins	Bake for 12 minutes or until a muffin springs back when pressed. Transfer to a wire rack to cool, then dust lightly with icing sugar.

I've included pancakes in this book mainly because they contain flour and when I was working in hotels these recipes, along with some tarts and pies, were still under the jurisdiction of the baker rather than the pastry chef.

This recipe is very simple to make and the pancakes are delicious served on a bed of cream with raspberry sauce rippled through it.

Sweet Treats

134

Pancakes with Bananas and Cream

250 g/8 oz white flour

30 g/1 oz caster sugar

1 egg

200 ml/7½ fl oz milk

60 ml/2½ fl oz sunflower oil

20 g/¾ oz butter

2 bananas, chopped

1 tablespoon dark rum

200 ml/7½ fl oz whipped cream

Serves 2

Whisk together the flour, 20 g/¾ oz of the sugar, the egg and milk for 5 minutes. You should now have a batter mixture. Test it by dipping a spoon in and seeing if it coats the back of the spoon evenly.

Heat a little sunflower oil in a frying pan and leave to smoke, then pour half a cup of the batter in the middle of the pan, tilt the pan to move the batter to the edges and replace on the heat for 3 minutes. Turn the pancake over with a spatula and fry for another 2 minutes. Remove from the pan and put on a plate to cool. Repeat with the rest of the batter.

To make the filling, drop the butter into the frying pan, add the bananas and cook for 1 minute. Add the rum and flambé until the flames die down. Cook for a further 2 minutes and leave to the side.

Whisk up the cream with the remaining sugar and spoon a little into the middle of each pancake. Top with the bananas, roll up and serve on a pool of pouring cream, if so desired – watch those waistlines!

My father and mother were both excellent at making pastry and I grew up knowing how to make good sweet pastry. Some pastry work is essential to becoming a good baker – it gives you a little edge on the competition.

I had this tart in Chinon in the Loire with a glass of Chablis for lunch, delicious!

Normandy Apple Tart

For the paste

375 g/13 oz strong white flour, plus extra for dusting

250 g/9 oz caster sugar

125 g/4 oz butter, softened

1 medium egg

splash of water to mix

4 dessert apples, thinly sliced

100 g/3½ oz apricot jam, warmed

For the frangipane

200 g/7 oz butter, softened

200 g/7 oz caster sugar

2 medium eggs plus 2 medium egg yolks

splash of calvados

60 g/2½ oz flour

200 g/7 oz ground almonds

Serves 8

Preheat the oven to 200°C/400°F/mark 6. To make the sweet paste, put the flour, sugar, butter, egg and water into a bowl and combine. Roll out on a lightly floured surface and use to line a 30.5 cm/12 inch shallow round cake tin.

To make the frangipane, cream the butter and sugar together and add the eggs and egg yolks one at a time. Add the Calvados, flour and ground almonds and mix well. Spread the frangipane over the paste in the cake ring, then fan out the apple slices from the edge to the middle in the form of a cross.

Bake for 25 minutes until golden brown. Brush with apricot jam while still warm and serve immediately.

My twist on the traditional recipe. The addition of real fruit lifts the pies to new heights. Remember when lining the moulds to keep the pastry thin and add plenty of filling.

Hollywood Mince Pies

For the pastry

375 g/13 oz strong white flour

250 g/9 oz butter, softened

125 g/4 oz caster sugar, plus extra for sprinkling

1 medium egg

splash of water to mix

For the filling

2 jars mincemeat

½ large tin of mandarins, drained and chopped

2 apples, finely diced

Makes 25 pies

Preheat the oven to 200°C/400°F/mark 6. To make the sweet pastry, rub the flour, butter, sugar and egg together with a splash of water to make a paste. If using a mixer, use the paddle and mix for 2 minutes. Do not overmix.

To make the filling, turn the mincemeat out into a bowl, throw the mandarins and apples into the bowl and blend in by hand.

Use deep muffin moulds. Rip off a small piece of sweet paste and line the sides and bottom of each mould. Fill each one with a good helping of the mincemeat mixture so that it reaches three-quarters of the way up the side of the mould.

Using a rolling pin, roll out your lids and cut to slightly bigger than the top of the moulds. Place a lid on top of each pie and gently push down. Prick the lids with a knife and sprinkle with sugar.

Bake for 20 minutes, then transfer to a wire rack to cool. Serve warm with fresh cream.

A very French recipe my mother-in-law is famous for. The cinnamon really adds another dimension to this pie.

I was first introduced to sweet paste by my mother Gill – she gave me this recipe and it's the best! The pastry will keep, covered in clingfilm, in the fridge for 1 week.

Apple Pie

Apple and Pear Pie with Fruit Sauce *Illustrated*

For the pastry

375 g/13 oz strong white flour

250 g/9 oz caster sugar

125 g/4 oz butter, softened

1 medium egg

100 g/3½ oz ground almonds

For the filling

1.4 kg/3 lb apples, peeled, cored and sliced

splash of Calvados

juice of 3 lemons

handful of sultanas

pinch of cinnamon

For the topping

1 egg, beaten, for eggwash

caster sugar, for sprinkling

Serves 6

Soak the sliced apples in the Calvados and lemon juice for 2 hours. Mix all the pastry ingredients together and leave to rest for 1 hour.

Preheat the oven to 200°C/400°F/ mark 6. Roll out the pastry to fit into a 30.5 cm/12 inch pie tin or foil base and fill with the apples and sultanas. Sprinkle with cinnamon. Roll out the pastry trimmings for the lid, cover the pie and crimp the edges together. Brush with the eggwash and sugar and bake for 25 minutes until golden brown.

For the pastry

375 g/13 oz strong white flour

250 g/9 oz caster sugar

125 g/4 oz butter, softened

1 medium egg

30 ml/1 fl oz water

For the filling

8 apples, peeled, cored and chopped

8 pears, peeled, cored and chopped

40 g/1½ oz sugar

For the topping

1 egg, beaten, for eggwash

caster sugar, for sprinkling

For the sauce

2 punnets raspberries

icing sugar

Serves 6

Preheat the oven to 200°C/400°F/ mark 6. To make the pastry, using a beater on an electric mixer, blend all the ingredients together to make a smooth pastry.

To make the filling, put the fruit and sugar into a pan and cook over a medium heat for 5 minutes to soften the fruit.

Roll the pastry out onto a 30.5 cm/ 12 inch pie plate and spoon on the filling. Roll out the excess pastry to make the lid and place on top. Trim the pastry edges and crimp around the edge, brush with eggwash and sprinkle with sugar. Bake for 25 minutes until golden brown.

Meanwhile make the raspberry sauce. Pass the raspberries through a sieve then stir in a little icing sugar. Serve with the pie.

Index